Just Between

You and Me

An Interactive Journal for Parents and Their Children

TRACY RUMPF

**Andrews McMeel
Publishing, LLC**
Kansas City

To my wonderful husband, Tim,
whose belief in me means so much.
Thank you for being such a loving husband and father.

To my four amazing children, Christopher, Kylie,
Brogan, and Brennan. I am so blessed to have you in my life,
and I cannot put into words how much I love all of you.
The four of you are truly the reason I was born.

07 08 09 10 11 TWP 10 9 8 7 6 5 4 3 2 1

ISBN-13: 978-0-7407-6548-3
ISBN-10: 0-7407-6548-5

www.andrewsmcmeel.com

Attention: Schools and Businesses
Andrews McMeel books are available at quantity discounts with bulk purchase for educational, business, or sales promotional use. For information, please write to: Special Sales Department, Andrews McMeel Publishing, LLC, 4520 Main Street, Kansas City, Missouri 64111.

Dear Moms and Dads,

Have you ever asked your child a question and gotten no response? Have you found at times that communicating with your tween or teenager is next to impossible? I think that at one time or another, all parents have been in this situation.

When my ten-year-old son starting having some problems at school, he did not want to talk about it. As much as it broke my heart that he wouldn't share his feelings with me, I knew I had to find a way to help him communicate his feelings. I bought a notebook and started writing down a few general questions about his feelings. We started writing back and forth to each other and before I knew it, he was opening up and telling me what was going on with him.

We began a journaling ritual. When I was finished writing I would put the notebook on my son's bed, and when he was finished writing he would put the notebook on my nightstand. We never verbally spoke about it; it was like we were part of a secret club and it was really fun. I began to do the same with my ten-year-old daughter, and I now feel that I have a good handle on what is going on in my children's lives. They start middle school this year, and in today's world, all parents need to find a way to communicate with their kids.

Here's how to use this journal:

Don't feel the need to write it in every day.

Typically at our house, we journal when there are problems, but we also journal about positive things. At least once a week I make sure to write how proud I am of them and point out the good things they are doing.

Included in the journal are resources such as Web sites you can refer to and lists of suggested conversation starters to help your journaling. Before you start, flip through the pages to find these resources.

Between You and Me is not only a way for you to communicate with your child, but it will also be a keepsake that you will have forever of the written thoughts and feelings between you and your child. What a wonderful gift to have!

Happy journaling,
Tracy Rumpf

Dear Kids,

You may be wondering what this journal is all about. A few years ago our mom started writing things to us in a notebook, asking us questions and telling us about her feelings as well. At first we thought it was just another one of Mom's ways to find out what was going on with us. She was always asking questions and kind of got on our nerves.

One day I (Christopher) came home from school and was not in a good mood. There was a kid in my class who was a bully, and he always tried to get me in trouble. He would say something or push me into the wall when the teacher wasn't looking. When I came home from school I guess my mom could tell that I was upset, but I didn't want to talk about it. Later that night when I was going to bed, I found a notebook on my pillow that had a question written on it. My mom asked me about what was going on with me and if she could help. Instead of me telling her, she told me I could write to her.

Since then, both of us write back and forth to our mom. There are days when we have nothing to say so we don't write. Sometimes we will find notes from both our mom and our dad telling us how proud they are of us or that we had a good game. It's pretty cool.

You may think this is kind of silly, but once you start, we think you will really like it. Sometimes there are things we want to talk about but don't want to say face to face. It's a lot easier to write down a question or what we are thinking. Some days when we see that our mom is upset or stressed out, we write to her, and she tells us that it helps her. That makes us feel really good.

Good luck and happy journaling,
Christopher and Kylie

dreams

are the touchstones of our character. : Henry David Thoreau

A Will Finds a Way

Seize the Moment

This Is **Your** Time

Happiness
is not a destination.
It is a method
of life.   : Burton Hills

Inspire · Dream · Create

Never let the
fear of the game keep you
from striking out.

The future belongs to those who believe in the beauty of their dreams.

: Eleanor Roosevelt

Dare to Be
Remarkable

Delight in Your Youth

Here are some **conversation starters** to discuss with your child. They are not always easy to talk about, but communication is such a necessity today.

★ What did you do in science (or another) class today?

★ What did you and your friends do at the game (concert, party)? Who was there?

★ What do you think about (a situation in the news)? How do you think you would handle the situation?

★ How do you feel about kids your age or kids in general using drugs (smoking, drinking, cheating, having sex, etc.)?

★ How do you feel when you see a kid at your school being pushed around or bullied?

★ How would you respond if someone asked you to do drugs or smoke cigarettes?

★ Remember to ask open-ended questions!

TOPICS

Friends • **Cheating and Lying**
Drugs and Alcohol • Beauty/Pressure to Be Thin
HIV and AIDS • Anorexia/Bulimia
Violence • Sexual Orientation
Bullying • **Popularity**
Teenage Pregnancy • Depression
Peer Pressure • Babysitting
Personal Hygiene • **Chores**
Relationships and Dating • Handling Stress
Car and Driving Safety • **Tobacco**
Huffing • Morals and Values
Weapons

This is my life. It is my one time to be me. I want to experience every good thing.

: Maya Angelou

Be Strong Be Happy

Be Wonderful

Be Yourself

Wonderful You

If you can *imagine* imagine it, you can achieve it. If you can *dream* dream it, you can become it.

: William A. Ward

Be Yo

Life is your canvas. No one
can paint it but you.

urself

It's a
Wonderful
World

Don't let anyone steal your dreams. Follow your heart no matter what.

: Jack Canfield

Follow Your *Destiny*

Free to Be Me!

Be True to Yourself

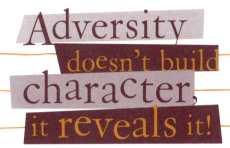

Adversity doesn't build character, it reveals it!

Imagine the Unimaginable

get real

If you want to be happy, BE.

: Leo Tolstoy

Every *moment* holds a hidden gift.

We create create our tomorrows by what we dream today.

Every step of the

journey

is the journey.

'The way to
know **life** is to know
many things.   : Vincent van Gogh

What do you see in the clouds?

I am here to live out loud.

: Emily Zola

I imagine,

therefore I belong and am free.

: Lawrence Durrell

Live Happy

Search *for* Your
Dreams

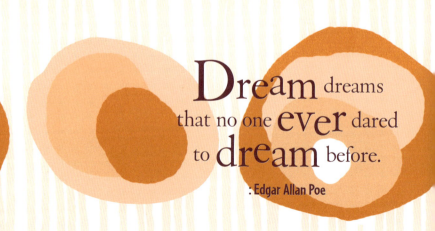

Dream dreams
that no one ever dared
to dream before.

: Edgar Allan Poe

Determination   Character   Confidence

The laughter of a child
is the light of a house.
: African Proverb

dreams

are the touchstones of our character. : Henry David Thoreau

A Will Finds a Way

Seize the Moment

This Is
Your
Time

Happiness
is not a destination.
It is a method
of life.
: Burton Hills

Inspire · Dream · Create

Never let the fear of the game keep you from striking out.

The **future** belongs to those
who **believe** in the beauty
of their **dreams**.

: Eleanor Roosevelt

Dare to Be
Remarkable

Delight in Your Youth

This is my life.
It is my one
time to be
me. I want to
experience
every good
thing.

: Maya Angelou

Be Strong   Be Happy

Be Wonderful

Wonderful You

If you can *imagine* imagine it, you can achieve it. If you can *dream* dream it, you can become it.

: William A. Ward

Be Yo

Life is your canvas. No one can paint it but you.

urself

It's a *Wonderful* World

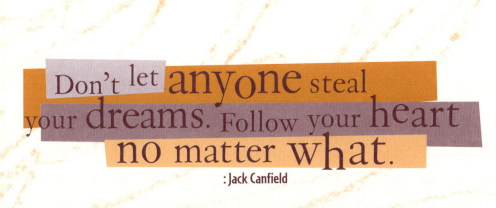

Don't let anyone steal your dreams. Follow your heart no matter what.

: Jack Canfield

Follow Your *Destiny*

Free to Be Me!

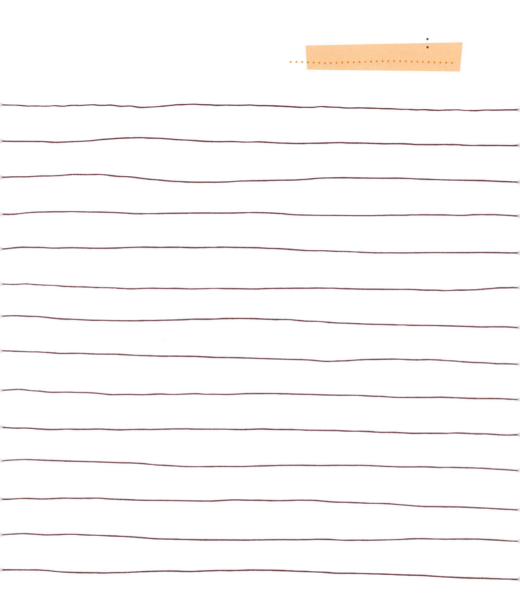

Be True to
Yourself

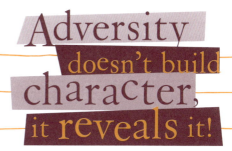
Adversity doesn't build character, it reveals it!

Imagine the

Unimaginable

get real

If you want to be happy, BE.

: Leo Tolstoy

Every *moment* holds a hidden gift.

We
create
create
our
tomorrows
by what
we dream
today.

GREAT WEB SITES

www.helpmyteen.com
www.allaboutyou.com
www.theantidrug.com
www.pbs.org/parents
www.pbskids.org
www.talkingwithkids.org
www.kidshealth.org
www.byparents-forparents.com
www.familiesaretalking.org
www.iparenting.com

Every step of the

journey

is the journey.

The way to
know **life** is to know
many things.   : Vincent van Gogh

What do you see in the clouds?

I am here
to live
out loud.

: Emily Zola

I imagine,

therefore I belong and am free.

: Lawrence Durrell

Live Happy

Search for Your *Dreams*

Dream dreams that no one ever dared to dream before.

: Edgar Allan Poe

Determination Character Confidence

The laughter of a child
is the light of a house.

: African Proverb

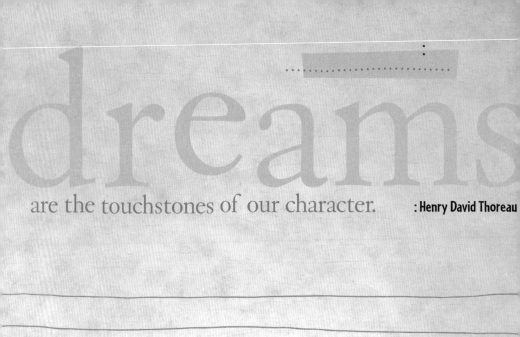

dreams

are the touchstones of our character.   : Henry David Thoreau

A Will Finds a Way

Seize the Moment

This Is **Your** Time

Happiness
is not a destination.
It is a method
of life.   : Burton Hills

Inspire · Dream · Create

Never let the
fear of the game keep you
from striking out.

The future belongs to those
who believe in the beauty
of their dreams.

: Eleanor Roosevelt

Dare to Be
Remarkable

Delight in Your Youth

This is my life.
It is my one
time to be
me. I want to
experience
every good
thing.
: Maya Angelou

Be Strong Be Happy

Be Wonderful

Be Yourself

Wonderful **Wonderful** You

If you can *imagine* imagine it, you can achieve it. If you can *dream* dream it, you can become it.

: William A. Ward

It's a

Wonderful
World

Be Yo

_____ :
....

Life is your canvas. No one
can paint it but you.

urself

dreams

are the touchstones of our character. : Henry David Thoreau

A Will Finds a Way

Seize *the* **Moment**

This Is **Your** Time

Happiness
is not a destination.
It is a method
of life.   : Burton Hills

Inspire · Dream · Create

Never let the
fear of the game keep you
from striking out.

The **future** belongs to those who **believe** in the beauty of their **dreams**.

: Eleanor Roosevelt

Dare to Be
Remarkable

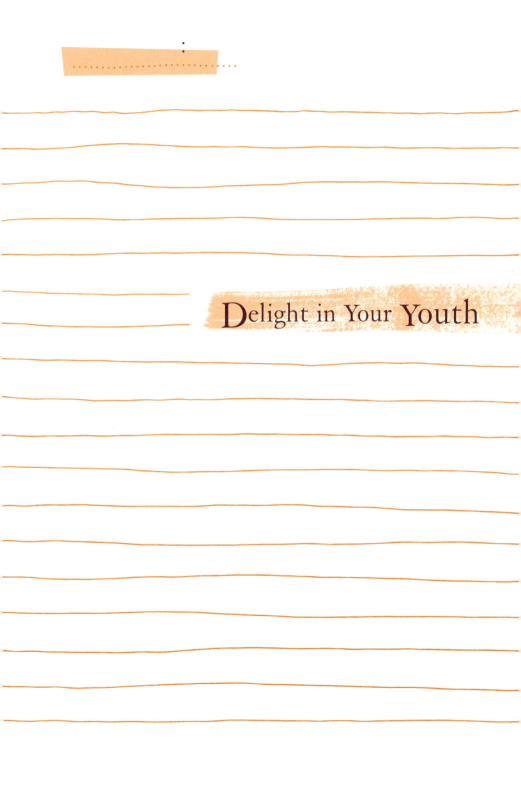

Delight in Your Youth

This is my life.
It is my one
time to be
me. I want to
experience
every good
thing.
: Maya Angelou

Wonderful You

Be Yo

Life is your canvas. No one can paint it but you.

urself

It's a
Wonderful
World

If you can *imagine* imagine it, you can achieve it. If you can *dream* dream it, you can become it.

: William A. Ward

Don't let anyone steal your dreams. Follow your heart no matter what.

: Jack Canfield

Follow Your *Destiny*

Free to Be Me!

Be true to

Yourself

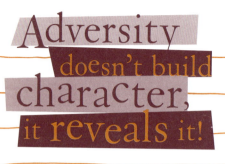

Adversity doesn't build **character,** it **reveals** it!

Imagine the

Unimaginable

get real

If you want to be happy, BE.

: Leo Tolstoy

EVERY *moment*
holds a hidden gift.

Pick Up a Book!

Who Put That Hair in My Toothbrush? by Jerry Spinelli

Crash by Jerry Spinelli

Number the Stars by Lois Lowry

Holes by Louis Sachar

The Giver by Lois Lowry

Walk Two Moons by Sharon Creech

Bud, Not Buddy by Christopher Paul Curtis

Everyday Ways to Raise Smart, Strong, Confident Girls by Barbara Littman

Too Old For This, Too Young for That! Your Survival Guide for the Middle-School Years by Harriet Mostache

Are You There God? It's Me, Margaret by Judy Blume

Inkheart by Cornelia Funke

Mickey and Me by Dan Gutman

A Wrinkle in Time by Madeleine L'Engle

The Complete Chronicles of Narnia by C. S. Lewis

Ballet Shoes by Noel Streatfeild

We create
create
our
tomorrows
by what
dream
we dream
today.

Every step of the

journey

is the journey.

The way to know **life** is **to** know many things.   : Vincent van Gogh

What do you see in the clouds?

I am here
to live
out loud.

: Emily Zola

I imagine,
therefore I belong and am free.

: Lawrence Durrell

Live Happy

Search *for* Your
Dreams

Dream dreams
that no one ever dared
to dream before.

: Edgar Allan Poe

Determination   Character   Confidence

The laughter of a child
is the light of a house.
: African Proverb

dreams

are the touchstones of our character.   : Henry David Thoreau

A Will Finds a Way

This Is
Your
Time

Happiness
is not a destination.
It is a method
of life.
: Burton Hills

Never let the fear of the game keep you from striking out.

The future belongs to those
who believe in the beauty
of their dreams.
: Eleanor Roosevelt

Dare to Be
Remarkable

Delight in Your Youth

This is my life. It is my one time to be me. I want to experience every good thing.

: Maya Angelou

Be Strong   Be Happy

Be Wonderful

Wonderful
Wonderful You

If you can *imagine* **imagine** it, you can achieve it. If you can *dream* **dream** it, you can become it.

: William A. Ward

Be Yo

Life is your canvas. No one can paint it but you.

urself

It's a Wonderful World

Don't let anyone steal your dreams. Follow your heart no matter what.

: Jack Canfield

Follow Your *Destiny*

Free to Be Me!

Be True to
Yourself

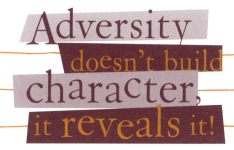

Adversity doesn't build character, it reveals it!

Imagine the

Unimaginable

get real

If you want to be happy, BE.

: Leo Tolstoy

Every *moment* holds a hidden gift.

We
create
create
our
tomorrows
by what
dream
we dream
today.

Every step of the

journey

is the journey.

The way to
know **life** is to know
many things.   : Vincent van Gogh

What do you see in the clouds?

I am here to live out loud.

: Emily Zola

I imagine,

therefore I belong and am free.

: Lawrence Durrell

Live Happy

Search for Your
Dreams

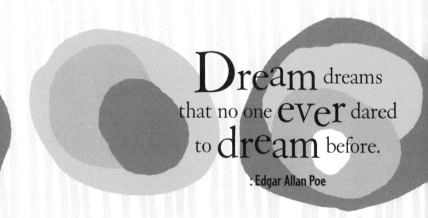

Dream dreams
that no one ever dared
to dream before.
: Edgar Allan Poe

Determination Character Confidence

The laughter of a child
            is the light of a house.
: African Proverb

dreams

are the touchstones of our character.   : Henry David Thoreau

A Will
Finds
a Way

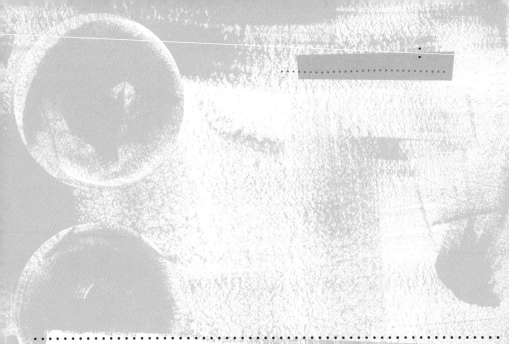

Promise Yourself

★ Promise yourself to be so strong that nothing can disturb your peace of mind.

★ To talk health, happiness, and prosperity to every person you meet.

★ To make all your friends feel like there is something in them.

★ To look at the sunny side of everything and make your optimism come true.

★ To think only of the best, to work only for the best, and expect only the best.

★ To be just as enthusiastic about the success of others as you are about your own.

★ To forget the mistakes of the past and press on to the greater achievements of the future.

★ To wear a cheerful countenance at all times and give every living person you meet a smile.

★ To give so much time to the improvement of yourself that you have no time to criticize others.

★ To be too large for worry, too noble for anger, too strong for fear, and too happy to permit the presence of trouble.

This Is Your Time

Happiness
is not a destination.
It is a method
of life.   : Burton Hills

Never let the
fear of the game keep you
from striking out.

The future belongs to those who believe in the beauty of their dreams.

: Eleanor Roosevelt

Dare to Be
Remarkable

Delight in Your Youth

This is my life.
It is my one
time to be
me. I want to
experience
every good
thing.
: Maya Angelou

Be Strong Be Happy

Be Wonderful

Be Yourself